# What Happens When I Sneeze?

By Madison Miller

**Gareth Stevens**
Publishing

Please visit our website, www.garethstevens.com. For a free color catalog of all our high-quality books, call toll free 1-800-542-2595 or fax 1-877-542-2596.

**Library of Congress Cataloging-in-Publication Data**

Miller, Madison
What happens when I sneeze / by Madison Miller
pg. cm. — (My body does strange stuff)
Includes index.
ISBN 978-1-4339-9343-5 (pbk)
ISBN 978-1-4339-9344-2 (6-pk)
ISBN 978-1-4339-9342-8 (library binding)
1. Sneezing—Juvenile literature. 2. Reflexes—Juvenile literature. I. Title.
QP123.8 M64 2014
612.2—dc23

Published in 2014 by
**Gareth Stevens Publishing**
111 East 14th Street, Suite 349
New York, NY 10003

Copyright © 2014 Gareth Stevens Publishing

Designer: Michael J. Flynn
Editor: Greg Roza

Photo credits: Cover, p. 1 Ian Boddy/Science Photo Library/Getty Images; p. 5 Paul Gregg/E+/Getty Images; p. 7 greenland/Shutterstock.com; p. 9 Alila Sao Mai/Shutterstock.com; p. 11 KidStock/Blend Images/Getty Images; p. 13 Jaimie Duplass/Shutterstock.com; p. 15 Jamie Wilson/Shutterstock.com; p. 17 © iStockphoto.com/BigPappa; p. 19 © iStockphoto.com/timsa; p. 21 (boy) matka_Wariatka/Shutterstock.com; p. 21 (girl) Nic Neish/Shutterstock.com.

Printed in the United States of America

CPSIA compliance information: Batch #CS13GS: For further information contact Gareth Stevens, New York, New York at 1-800-542-2595.

# Contents

**Boldface** words appear in the glossary.

# Ah...Ah...CHOO!

It happens to everyone. You feel a tickle in your nose. You rub your nose, but the tickle gets stronger. Soon, your body takes in a quick breath and—AHCHOO! Sneezing is our body's way of blasting **germs** and **irritants** out of the nose.

5

# Drip Drip Drip

When germs or irritants enter the nose, the nose releases special **chemicals**. These chemicals tell the body that something is there that shouldn't be. They can make the eyes and nose get watery. They also make the nose itch.

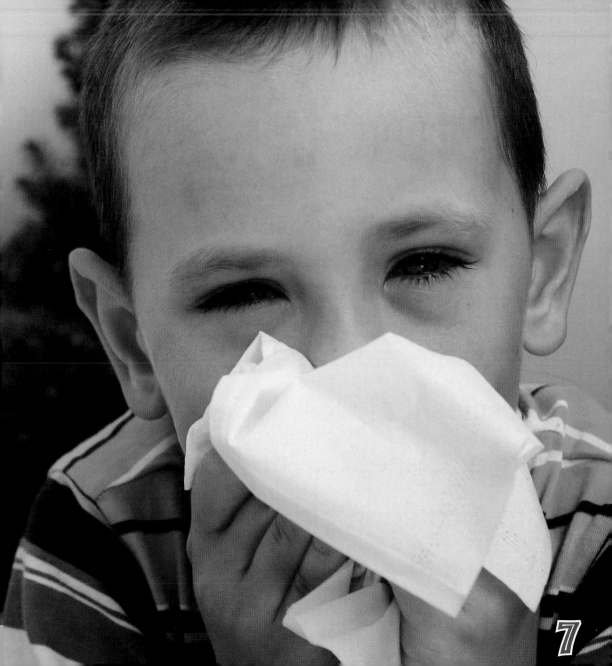

## Nerves and Muscles

When we feel an itch inside our nose, **nerves** send a message to the brain. The brain then sends the message out to all the **muscles** that work together to make us sneeze. Those muscles are located in the belly, chest, neck, and head.

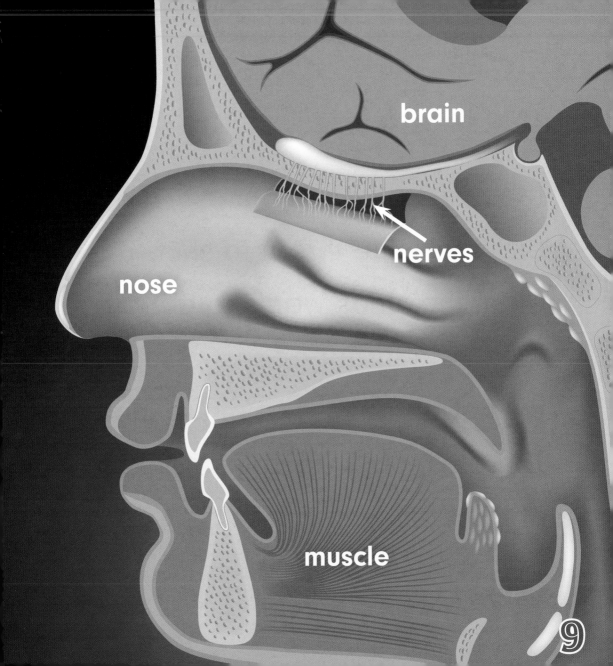

## Let It Out

Moments before a sneeze, the brain tells the throat to shut. The air in the lungs wants to get out. When the throat opens, a sudden rush of air bursts out of the lungs. The blast of air forces irritants out of the throat and nose.

11

# Why We Sneeze

Many things can make us sneeze. Dust is one of the most common kinds of irritants. Smoke can make us sneeze, too. Maybe you've sneezed while putting pepper on your food. All these things can tickle the inside of your nose.

When you catch a cold, germs grow inside your body. Some even grow inside your nose! To fight these germs, the body releases special chemicals. These chemicals cause **mucus** to collect. Our body sneezes to get rid of the mucus and germs.

People with allergies get sick from things that don't normally make other people sick. These things include dust and pets. People with allergies often sneeze a lot, even though they don't really need to. That's because their nose itches and creates a lot of mucus.

17

# Cover Up!

A sneeze can travel 100 miles (160 km) per hour! That's fast enough to send anything in your nose flying. It's important to cover your mouth and nose when you sneeze. That will stop you from spreading germs—or getting mucus on your friends!

19

## Light Sneezing?

Did you know that some people sneeze when looking at a bright light? Bright light affects nerves in the eyes, which can cause a similar reaction in the nearby nerves of the nose. This leads to a sneeze or even a fit of sneezing!

CAUSES OF SNEEZING

colds

allergies

irritants

bright light

dust

smoke

21

# Glossary

**chemical:** matter that can be mixed with other matter to cause changes

**germ:** a tiny creature that can cause illness

**irritant:** something that causes discomfort to the body

**mucus:** slimy stuff that keeps the inside of your body safe

**muscle:** one of the parts of the body that allow movement

**nerve:** a part of the body that carries messages to and from the brain and allows us to feel things

# For More Information

## Books

Durant, Penny. *Sniffles, Sneezes, Hiccups, and Coughs.* New York, NY: DK Publishing, 2005.

Minden, Cecilia. *Keep It Clean: Achoo!* Ann Arbor, MI: Cherry Lake, 2010.

## Websites

### KidsHealth
*kidshealth.org/kid*
Find more information about sneezing and many other health topics.

### Sneezing
*www.cyh.com/HealthTopics/HealthTopicDetailsKids. aspx?p=335&np=152&id=2666*
Read much more about sneezing, including how people in Japan say "ahchoo"!

# Index